Memories Of Brackley

Memories Of Brackley

A Millennium Project

By

Brackley 50+ Club

Date of Publication: October 1999
Reprinted: March 2004

Published by:
Brackley 50+ Club

Printed by:
ProPrint
Riverside Cottage
Great North Road
Stibbington
Peterborough PE8 6LR

ISBN: 0 9537046 0 2

Aerial view of Brackley 1960

CONTENTS:

INTRODUCTION

This is not a history book nor just a source of information about our town. Yet Memories of Brackley is both historical and informative, and we hope, evocative and amusing, with tales of our past that will interest newcomers and old inhabitants alike.

Thanks are due to all our 50+ Club members who contributed to this book. We would like to thank others who helped.

Cover design by Robert Pell

Articles by   Caryl Billingham
                    Suzanne Billingham
                    Eddie Palmer
                    John Clarke
                    Mike Barlow
                    Colin Miller
                    Anne Steedman
                    Mike Cassford

and to Indrani Gleave for help and advice.

Mary Yates
Brackley 50+ Club

Grant Aided by South Northamptonshire Council through their Millennium Grants Scheme.

Postscript 2004:

This is a re-issue of our book. We sold 700 copies of the first issue.

A BYGONE AGE

I was born here in Brackley in the mid 1920s when it was a busy, thriving, little market town with a population of just over 2000.

The town itself was the one long main street as today, entered at the south end past the Gas Light and Coke Company, and then the L.M.S. Railway, ending exactly one mile on by passing the L.N.E.R. station, and from the early thirties the Sawmills.

Ribbon Development had begun on Halse Road and Banbury Road, Buckingham Road could not be built on below the Croft due to shifting sands.

Manor Road known then as Back Way was as its name suggests the back entrance to most of the High Street properties. It had no surface water drains and at storm times High Street properties were often flooded. I well remember my home, a farm house, being flooded inches deep and the cellar had to be pumped out by the fire brigade. We children were sent to an Aunt's house on Banbury Road until it was dried out. We loved going there as we did a good impression of the Railway Children, sitting on the wall at the bottom of the garden and waving to the driver and the passengers of the trains toing and froing from Banbury.

Banbury Road itself could only be built so far on one side due to the land dropping sharply and always being very wet. On the other side it continued to the Workhouse (Now West Hill Gardens). It was a large building of which I know little, but one memory is of the hospital ward there for terminally ill patients. My Grandfather was one of these and on visiting (I was about eight years old) the peace and cleanliness remains vivid in my mind. A highly polished floor and a little chapel with a beautiful stained glass window I also remember.

Old Town and St Peter's were there but much alteration to housing in the area has been done. Gone are the yards of cottages and rows of cottages which housed so many people in that area. More recently the old vicarage has also been demolished.

Brackley was renowned for its educational standards and many children from all over the world boarded at Magdalen

College, The Girls High School and Winchester House School. Apart from this, hundreds of children arrived by train at both stations and returned home at night. Who said our trains were not used? Men commuted to London and other places to work and were greatly inconvenienced when the lines closed. Feed my Lambs School which I attended holds many memories not least the nature walks taken around the area. One such was around Turweston and on the return journey a thunder storm blew up. Rather than get thirty plus children soaked we were all passed into the built up sections of the viaduct. The walls were about two feet thick and the ground inside sloped steeply. Here we had a singing lesson to drown the noise of the storm and had the thrill of a train going over high above us. Another memory was going to Aldershot Tattoo, courtesy of Miss Beatrice Cartwright, leaving in the dark, and returning in the dark, it was so much enjoyed. From the playground we watched the felling of the very large tree which stood in the Market Place outside what is known as Boots, we marvelled at the size of the trunk as it was brought past the school on a horse drawn timber wagon. On Armistice Day we were all taken to the Market Place for the service at the War Memorial. The Grafton Hunt always met at the same time and moved off only after taking part in the service and a stirrup cup provided by Lord Penryhn of Brackley house.

Every September Mr Wilson brought his fair to the town, much, much, bigger than today. He always came to the school and talked about the new rides etc. and gave every child tickets for two rides.

I remember a Sunday School outing to Brighton; we caught the train at the Bottom Station and the great thrill of being shunted at Bletchley to join another train. Later outings were always to Wickstead Park at Kettering where we always saw to it that the Vicar got soaked.

The Park

This was gifted to the National Trust by the Earl of Ellesmere to ensure that the views from the Manor House were never built up. It was open to the public in the summer months, locked up at the end of October and sheep grazed it through the winter. When these were taken out usually in March it remained closed for a cut of hay to be taken before being open to the public again around Ascension Day.

It had swings, see-saw and sandpit for children positioned well away from the road.

The Fire Brigade practised in there during the evening attracting lots of onlookers and childish hopefuls. The ornate Iron Panel was put in the wall when it was given to the town by the family of Clarke and Sons who made it at their Ironmongery business, now Burgess in the Market Square; it had for many years been fixed to the front of their showroom as a demonstration piece.

Park Hospital

This was as the name suggests opposite the park in what is now Park Lodge and the Dentist. It was a seventeen bed hospital housed in what had been Dr Stathers' family home and surgery. It was open for about ten years finally closing in May 1945. It was always full and the men's ward on the ground floor was often taken over for women. Operations were carried out by surgeons from Oxford and Northampton. I remember one op in my early days at the hospital. It was on a very large lady who fortunately had an equally large sense of humour. She walked to the theatre from her upstairs ward and when the time came for her to go back to the ward the surgeon asked how she was going back. Dr Stathers immediately said 'Oh the girls will carry her'. 'Not on your life!' said the surgeon, who rang for the Fire Brigade, who in turn carried her back up the ornate and turning staircase with quite a degree of difficulty.

Happy days were many working there, matron's wedding being one. Her gift from the staff was an Apple Pie Bed for which we were not popular. At one stage we were issued with a new uniform (gold dust in those days) but we were sworn to secrecy and it must not be worn until we were told. Later we discovered that the Duchess of Gloucester had chosen Park Hospital as the second choice when the present Duke was born. She was booked in at Northampton Nursing Home but had anything gone wrong i.e. early or late delivery she was coming to us. What an honour!

Shops

Shops were many and varied not only around the Market Square but also in middle of the Square and other parts of the town as well.

The decline of the shops was not caused by the arrival of supermarkets, it started in the 60s when the Market Square was ruined. The chemist shop facing the Town hall was demolished. It had stood there from the 1600s and was then known as the Doctor's House. All traces of the market went, pens, weighbridge etc. and the most beautiful town house on Banbury Road corner also went. Several shops had two sales floors and you did not have to go out of town to buy anything. We had three bespoke tailors, milliners, furnishers, clothing, jewellers, newsagents florists etc.

The one thing that is worth noting was the unrelated names of the shops, Salmon - Butcher, Plumb - Fishmonger, Plank - Baker, Sandles - Baker, Wood - Grocer. Also in the square was a riding school - now Draymans Walk which was very popular in pre-war days. Blencowes Brewery finished in the 20s, vinegar and marmalade were two things made for a short time on the site before the riding school was established.

Hopcroft and Norris brewery on the other side of the square continued under varying management until I think the 60s when Bronnley's Soap bought the site and employed many local people. One small shop of note was owned by a Mrs Moss, it was the front room of her house next door to the Fox on the Banbury Road. Mr Moss followed his own job as Postman, Town Hall Keeper and Mace Bearer and also rang the curfew bell at eight pm at the Town Hall every evening. I well remember visiting Mrs Moss after her husband had died and she had closed her shop. She very proudly showed me the linoleum which had been moved down from the bedroom above. She had the receipt from its purchase in May 1933 from Hatwells in the Market Square at 6d a square yard and this was in the 60s. She was very proud and rightly so of her grandson the singer Ralph McTell who visited her quite regularly.

Away from the Market Square and also the High Street were several shops which hold memories for me. Four shops on the site of the P.O. Sorting Office and Pizza Shop, Newbury's Cycles, Booth Taxi and Furniture Removals Office, The London Central Meat Company Butchers Shop and a small chemist shop. This was run by Mrs Merry who had been Matron at Park Hospital. The counter was quite high and she was short in stature but so friendly with everyone, all the children who went into the shop were given Jelly Babies and if they had fallen and grazed their knees, hands etc. she cleaned and dressed their wounds at no charge. She kept a supply of plasters with pictures on, smiling faces, matchstick men etc. which cured many tearful episodes. The shop sign was truly as it said *A MERRY CHEMIST.* The Oak Cottage Cafe was always popular and Turners Grocers Shop opposite to it was noted for freshly ground coffee which was roasted in the cellar with a trap door at pavement level to let out the fumes, a wonderful smell!

The market was purely a cattle market held every Monday morning in the year with the exception of the first Monday in December when it was the Fat Stock Show known as the Old Fair. Hay wagons were lined up in the centre of the square hurdles attached to the wheels, straw was spread along by these and the cattle according to class tied to them. Sheep were penned along Burgess side of the square, pigs and calves in the permanent building in the sales yard -now Highfield Court. Two retail stalls came on this day. One sold all kinds of home-made rock and the other known as Cheap Jack sold crockery.

The town boasted three brass bands The Town Band, The Silver Band - both prize winners in their time and The Salvation Army who held their outdoor service on the hard shoulder by the Greyhound, then paraded through the town to their barracks in Halls Lane. The Hollywood Dance Band was another group who were very much sort after. They were mainly the Alcock family and their friends who filled a local need.

Wartime Brackley

Plans were made and approximately two thousand evacuees were brought to Brackley by train and homes found in the surrounding villages as well as the town. They came mainly from

Marylebone, Chingford and Whitechapel areas. Some stayed through out the war and still have contact to this day.

Many airfields were built all around the town and the army stationed actually in the town using every available space, building etc. including the Railway Station.

Bakelite Ltd moved their H.Q. to Brackley taking Brackley Lodge. Their staff came with them and lived among the locals, also lots of jobs were created for local girls in the offices.

We were very fortunate in as much as we had only one lot of bombs dropped in the vicinity, along the new concrete drive to Brackley Grange. Ironically this had been laid when Ribbentrop visited to open Croughton Airfield just before the war. Maybe it was mistaken for the runway, but in any case what a thank you to Wing Commander James for his hospitality; he lived at the Grange. The last bomb from this stick fell in gardens in Evenley.

NAAFI had a unit in the High Street which was always busy (more news of this from Gwyn Jones whose parents were in charge and he was brought up there).

A silly memory of a previous Mayor's Sunday. The parade was from the Town Hall to St Peter's with all organisations and schools taking part. The mayor and councillors followed the band on foot. It was on the return march opposite the park when the Mayor's (Miss B. Cartwright) knickers descended round her ankles. She stepped out, hung them on her arm and continued with the parade. This was typical of her and her personality. A great benefactor to the town.

Mary Jukes.

THE COUNCIL

When I was a child Brackley was a borough: it was its own planning authority, it owned and managed its own council houses, it had its own public health department and staff.

Indeed, Brackley had been a borough for so long - under various charters, mostly royal but the first from Simon de Montfort and Roger de Quincey (I think) - that in 1960 it celebrated its seven hundredth anniversary. As a nine year old I remember principally the street parties. But we did have a royal visit from the Duke and Duchess of Gloucester, and the Brackley borough council did give the freedom of the borough to the Northamptonshire Yeomanry and we did have an ox roast in the Market Square where of course in those days there was still a weekly cattle market.

In 1973, under local government reorganisation, it was decreed that Brackley would lose its borough status and that the Brackley Rural District Council which served the surrounding villages and had its offices in Brackley (at Brackley Lodge now being renovated by Mullion Limited) would be subsumed into the new South Northamptonshire District Council. The local council in Brackley handed over nearly all of its assets - council houses, land etc. even the swimming pool after a couple of years - and assumed the status of only a Parish Council. As the former borough, however, we were allowed to style ourselves a Town Council.

However, we do now have very little power or authority. We own and run the Town Hall and the cemetery; we maintain the park which is owned by the National Trust. The Market Place, effectively highway, is ours to run, therefore so are the market and the annual fair. We are consulted on all planning matters which are submitted to the district council as planning authority, and our opinions are carefully considered during the decision-making process. To a large extent, we act as a pressure group for other agencies because we are at the grass roots; we **miss** the litter bins which the district council should replace; we **report** the non-functioning street-lamps which need to be repaired by others, and so on.

So, when someone tells you it's 'the council', it might not be us, the Town Council. in fact, it most probably isn't, but it is most likely the Town Council that gets the message through effectively and efficiently to the right agency so that work can be carried out as quickly as possible. Or, as they say, '...but I know a man who can.'

Caryl Billingham
Town Mayor.

BRACKLEY COTTAGE HOSPITAL

In 1961 Brackley was a quiet little market town with a population of approximately three thousand five hundred.

It had its own railway station with direct lines to the north and south; London being only a one hour journey away.

I came here to become Matron of The Cottage Hospital in Pebble Lane, aptly named, as it used to be a lane made up of pebbles.

From the outside, the hospital looked like a row of cottages, with a lovely lavender hedge; roses, winter jasmine and japonica adorned the walls. There were two very prolific holly bushes, plus two small flower beds. Quite picturesque.

The front door was on the side of the building and opened on to a long corridor, with cherry red and mustard coloured linoleum tiles. I was struck by the lovely warm atmosphere which I found very welcoming.

As Mr Donald Smith, Physiotherapist has already published a very comprehensive and interesting book entitled Brackley Cottage Hospital, I will give you some of my memories.

Running a Cottage Hospital is very similar to managing a big home. I was responsible for my own budget. I had to endeavour to keep everyone happy and satisfied.

Happy memories.

Christmas

Christmas was an especially lovely time. Christmas trees were supplied from the sawmills. Everywhere was decorated and stockings filled for patients and staff.

I got up early and dressed as Father Christmas, gave out the presents.

The Vicar began the day with a Holy Communion Service and later, the doctors and their families came to wish the patients a happy day. Also, the Mayor and Mayoress.

Dr Thomas, who lived opposite the Hospital, came to carve the turkey and everyone was offered a glass of sherry.

Christmas crackers, a gift from Miss Smart, were pulled and festive hats worn.

Mrs Hilda Keen, Cook did extra cooking for Christmas e.g. ham, tongue, pork pies, sausage rolls, mince pies, Christmas puddings and cakes. What a lovely aroma pervaded the building.

Easter

Easter was another special time. Presents of new laid eggs were brought in from the town and neighbouring villages. All the patients and staff had a chocolate egg.

Harvest Festival

Very exciting! Baskets of fruit and vegetables kept arriving from local schools and churches. These were sorted and stored in a hut in the garden.

NB. This was a revolving hut used to home patients with Tuberculosis. (Now not required thank goodness).

Other Events

Other events include the pancake race and carnival, with staff participating where possible. One glorious summer, the staff prepared a float but on the big day, the skies opened! But they still had fun!

Births

Everyone was thrilled to see a new-born baby, bathed and dressed with hair suitably styled. A real tonic for the general patients especially if they were allowed to touch the baby and maybe cross its palm with silver.

Deaths

When I was shown a small wooden hut in the garden and told that it was the mortuary, in my innocence I thought of maybe the odd stillborn baby. I soon came to realise that this building could accommodate four to five bodies at a time!

Nursing staff had to perform last offices, and convey the body on a trolley up to the shed. Very hazardous in bad weather. Later the local undertaker took the deceased to their chapel of rest and was responsible for the laying out.

Heating

This was a coke boiler in the cellar. The staff were responsible for keeping this going when the handyman/gardener was off duty. A very dirty job! Later it was changed to an oil fired boiler with a big tank in the garden. What a wonderful day when the tank was dismantled and carried away and gas installed.

Weather

This being England, we had to be prepared for all eventualities. Severe storms were often responsible for water to come flooding into the hospital. Then it was a case of all hands on deck to mop up.

In 1963 and 1965 and later, snowstorms were particularly bad with villages being cut off and snow as high as the hedge in Helmdon Road. My loyal staff never let me down. one Staff Nurse walked in from Sulgrave and another from Thenford. The Vicar arrived for the Sunday service on a sledge and some maternity patients had to come in by tractor.

1976 - Centenary Year

The Physiotherapy unit was upgraded. The whole building was replaced so Mr Smith had to use a small room just inside the hospital. it was a big relief when he could move into his new building.

The League Of Friends

The League of Friends had managed to raise enough money to upgrade the Maternity Department providing a nursery and modern labour ward.

Wootton Bros. were given the contract to perform this mammoth task and proved first class. The weather got hotter and hotter but still the workmen toiled with their dusty job. But at last, all was complete and we were able to open the new wing. What a happy day!

We celebrated our special year with a Church Service of Thanksgiving and had an open day with refreshments to show off our new building.

Hygiene

Because of the close proximity of the General and Maternity patients, strict hygiene had to be observed. Nursing staff were responsible for disinfecting beds and wards with special attention to the Casualty and Labour wards.

One Nursing Auxiliary came back on a voluntary basis every Saturday to spring clean the Labour ward.

Matron's Duties

As I had no secretary, I was responsible for all my office work including correspondence. I made a point of acknowledging all letters and gifts.

In spite of repeated threats of closure, Brackley Hospital is still functioning now under a new title. Unfortunately, we lost the Maternity beds in 1986.

The warm welcome is still there which is wonderful considering all the changes.

May it long continue.

Delia Frost.

HALSE

If you are considering the history of Brackley you should include the history of Halse. I understand that the initial settlement in this area was at Halse, and only later did it move a couple of miles to what is now Old Town, Brackley.

There was a Manor at Halse, located where Manor Farm now stands, earlier this century all the land around here would appear to have been owned by the Earl of Ellesmere. It was through his good offices that both the land and the Halse Mission building were presented to the residents of Halse to enable them to hold religious services in their area.

The Mission building a Tin Tabernacle was originally erected in Brackley for the use of navvies building the Brackley viaduct. When the task was completed, the Earl of Ellesmere purchased the building and arranged for it to be re-erected in its present position on his land, at the beginning of the Halse residential area.

The building was dedicated on the 28th October 1909 and has been in continuous use ever since for both church services and village hall purposes.

When the Earl of Ellesmere's estate were wound-up in 1923 the land and building was transferred to the diocese of Peterborough for the sum of ten shillings, copies of this agreement are still available.

Whilst Brackley continued to develop and grow, little happened at Halse, being occupied by only the four farms and the staff required to run them.

Then in the early 1970s Mr Kibble the then owner of many of the farms and land, decided to sell off small plots for building on both sides of the Brackley to Greatworth Road, hence the present level of development in this area.

Frank Bridge.

CHARLES CLARKE AND THE TOP STATION

Brackley's Top Station opened in 1899 and closed in 1966. Today, some of the buildings still survive as a tyre depot. The change in use symbolises the victory of road over rail transport which has transformed this country over the past forty years. But, at least in Brackley, the victory is not total. Many of those who go to change their tyres or have their exhausts replaced, remember the station as it was. I suspect that as they wait, quite a few half expect to see a plume of smoke or hear the whistle of a steam locomotive.

It was a large and very handsome station; its red and purple bricks were lightly glazed and resisted weathering so well that, right to the end, it had a new, slightly raw look. It was designed by Alexander Ross, a Scotsman from Inverness. Even before I knew anything about the architect, I fancied the station had something of a Scottish feel about it; perhaps it was all those fir trees, or perhaps it was because it always seemed so cold. The life of the station focused around the few warm spots. On the platform, a large brazier was placed under the water column to prevent the water from the engines freezing up. Sometimes - though many thought not often enough - a small fire was lit in the General Waiting Room. There was usually a better fire in the tiny Porter's Room under the bridge. But the most important source of heat was the stove in the Booking Office which thus made it the 'social centre' of the station. It was there that my father, Charles Clarke, worked and where favoured passengers were allowed to warm themselves while waiting for their trains. The station had a unique smell, a mixture of coal, engine smoke, gas - and it remained gas-lit to the end - glue for fixing the posters, and the disinfected sawdust dressing regularly applied to the parquet floor of the entrance hall and Booking Office. Built for the Great Central Railway, its official name was Brackley Central Station - even though it was actually at the extreme northern end of town.

Although there were two stations in Brackley - the other was on the branch line from Bletchley to Banbury - the Top Station, with direct connection to London and the North, was the more important. In the days before near universal car ownership and the general expansion of road transport, the Top Station played a crucial role in Brackley's economic and social life. Then goods and people went by train. Incoming parcels were distributed first on horse drays and later on the dray pulled by a 'mechanical horse', driven by Bob Philips. Most people bought their coal from merchants based at the station - Price Summers, Welfords or Frosts. The station was also a place where visitors had their first impressions of Brackley - whether frightened little boys about to start boarding at Winchester House or Magdalen or grandees bound for one of the 'big houses' in the neighbourhood.

My own direct memories of the station cover its last phase when it was already in the hands of its third owner - the first was the Great Central, the second, in 1923 the L.N.E.R., and the last, in 1948, British Railways. It was from there that I took my first train journey at the age of three in 1950. As a child in the 1950s, I was a regular visitor to the station, an eager trainspotter, who loved the atmosphere of the place but, especially in later years, regretted that there were so few trains and that these always seemed to be pulled by the same engines. I really got fed up with seeing 76044 and 73157 day after day. Some of the other trainspotters got up to all sorts of mischief, but I could not; I was under the watchful eye of my father in the Booking Office.

Great Central Station, Brackley

My father died in September 1998 at the age of 87, more than thirty years after the station saw its last train. He never wrote down his memories of the railway and that is a pity - he knew more about the station than I do and his prose style was much superior. He came to work at the station in 1946, but his links went back much earlier. At the time of his birth, in the middle of the scorching summer of 1911, his father, another Charles Clarke, was a signalman at Brackley. Born in Banbury, my grandfather first served on the Great Western but around the turn of the century transferred to the Great Central - a change of allegiance for which his brother, Ernest a guard on the Great Western, never quite forgave him. At first, he was a shunter at Leicester, but following an accident, became a signalman and arrived in Brackley shortly before my father's birth. Over the years, he worked with men like Charlie Blencowe and Reg Hinson. Although my grandfather retired at the end of World War II, Reg carried on working in the box. In the days of post-war labour shortages, he was kept on till he was over seventy. My grandfather would sometimes take me to the signal box when Reg was on duty. Brackley Box, like others on the Great Central, was always immaculate. Signalmen never pulled a lever with their bare hands - that would have left finger marks on the shining metal. A tea towel or duster was always used. At Brackley, the brown linoleum floor was so highly polished that it was positively dangerous. Signalmen were obsessed with their floors, even to the extent of regarding slipping on their linoleum and breaking a leg as an appropriate culmination to their careers; this distinction was later achieved by 'Gus' Torrance.

When my father left Magdalen College School in 1926, he joined the L.N.E.R. as a clerk. In those days a job 'in railway service' was much sought after and, remarkably, candidates for clerical posts had to take an examination which included papers in French and Latin. Between then and joining the army in 1940 my father worked at a number of stations on the line, including Whetstone, Leicester, Finmere and Calvert, but he knew most of the staff at Brackley. They included the Station Master, Mr Taylor, a bachelor who sang bass in the Church Choir, George Knibbs, the Porter with such a loud voice that when he called out 'Brackley,

Brackley' as the trains arrived in the station, he could be heard at the Bell, and Jimmy Hume, the Booking Clerk, a rather nervous man who had had a rough time as a prisoner of the Germans in World War I. Jimmy had been in the Royal Corps of Signals, the Regiment to which most railway clerks were attached - because they were believed to be good at Morse code. When the Second World War came, my father, too, was sent into the Royal Corps of Signals. By this time, railway clerks actually spoke to other stations by telephone and had largely forgotten Morse, but news of this development had not reached the military authorities.

When World War II ended, my father became a Booking Clerk at Brackley - in every sense of the word it was like coming home. Of course, things had changed during the war; now there were women in the Booking Office. One was a Miss Snowball, a very shy lady, easily embarrassed and prone to blushes. Local youths would torment her with fictitious enquiries about trains to stations with rude sounding names - 'how much is a third class return to Piddle Hinton please?' My father soon put a stop to that. When he came back to Brackley, the Station Master was Mr Franklin, regarded by many as a stern disciplinarian and not greatly liked by many of the staff, including my grandfather. In his early years, Franklin, whose family came from Westbury, had been a union activist, but was now very much 'the company's man'. But my father got on well with him - perhaps because they had worked together earlier at Calvert before the war. When Miss Snowball left she was replaced by the Station Master's daughter-in-law, the former Daphne Howard, who was married to Arthur Franklin, a Porter at the station.

In the early post war years, the station was still busy and, by modern standards, there was a very large staff - a Station Master, two Booking Clerks, three Passenger Porters ('Bluey' Spencer, 'Tidler' Faulkner and Arthur Franklin), a Goods Agent (Nelson Coles), a Goods Clerk (Tom Billingham), two Goods Porters, a Drayman and three Signalmen. Station Masters came and went - Mr Franklin retired to Rugby and was replaced by Mr Beech, who in turn was replaced by Bob Smith. Smith was a jolly cockney, full of good humour and prone to slightly risqué jokes. He had started life on the old Great Eastern Railway, which was considered a rather 'common' company by Great Central men who prided themselves on their - comparative - gentility. Smith tended to spend his mornings, not at the station, but in the Conservative Club. He argued, perhaps rightly, that as the railway's chief representative in the town, he needed to get out and about to bring attention to all the wonderful services - holidays, excursions and special deals - that the then Eastern Region of British Railways could offer. He was positively lyrical on the delights of 'Bracing Skegness' as a holiday resort.

It was in Bob Smith's time that the station enjoyed an Indian summer. The flaking grey paint left over from the war years was replaced by the British Railways crimson lake and cream. It was suspected however that not all of the paint was used at the station and it was remarkable how many Brackley people decided to paint their houses red and cream around 1954. In those days there was a good service with fast trains hauled by Gresley A3 Pacifics and V2s in Brunswick Green BR livery. Above all the Booking Office usually seemed crowded with people. One virtual fixture was the taxi-driver Herbie Hitchcock, particularly anxious to be of service to the American airmen based at Croughton - generous with their tips and gifts of PX cigarettes and whisky. Then there were the local grandees - General Bradshaw of Turweston, Colonel Smiley of Brackley Grange and the rather fierce Brigadier Manton, who had been in the Royal Corps of Transport and who regularly wrote to the Station Master to express his 'vexation' when trains were late. On occasion there was a figure from an earlier age, the elderly and charming Lady Birkenhead, widow of Lord Chancellor Birkenhead, whose funeral in 1929 had brought to the station some of its most distinguished visitors, including Winston Churchill.

In the 1930s it was said that 'The business of Brackley is education' and 'education' still dominated the life of the station in the 1950s. The largest single category of passengers were the boys and girls, pupils at Magdalen or the High School, who came in daily from Woodford, Culworth and Helmdon. Of course, they were not let into the Booking Office, but teachers were. There were many boarding schools in Brackley and the surrounding area and their pupils also travelled by train, providing good business for the station. Brackley stole a march on nearby Buckingham by 'capturing' the special train put on from London at the beginning of each term to bring the boys back to Stowe. Some of the most regular visitors to the Booking Office stove were the Headmasters or representatives of boarding establishments who came to make arrangements for their pupils' transport - Eric Forrester of Magdalen, Mr Llewellyn of Winchester House, Mr Atkins, the Bursar of Stowe and Mr Clark of Evenley Hall. With all of these my father formed life long friendships. They would sit talking, sometimes drinking tea, under the racks of tickets. There was quite a lot of money in the tills under the counter and my father would be asked what he would do if there was a robbery. He would take from a drawer a large truncheon with a lead weight inserted at the end; fortunately it was never needed.

Brackley Station was proud of its gardens and often won prizes. But the pièce de résistance was the goldfish pond. The pond was created from a former flower bed and fed with water from the adjacent 'Gents'. It was the special pride and joy of Tom Billingham. I still have nightmares about the things that Tom threatened to do to anyone who interfered with his fish. The pond caught the attention of an occasional visitor to the station, the poet John Betjeman, a man who loved railways and especially anything 'quirky' connected with them. Betjeman said he was 'enchanted' by the goldfish pond. I think he toyed with the idea of writing a poem about it - it would have been wonderful if he had.

John Betjeman was not the only famous poet to come to the Top Station. Even in the 1950s the station seemed to be living in something of a 'time warp' - a Victorian or Edwardian one. There was one passenger, however who 'stretched' the time warp much further back into the past. Perhaps the most extraordinary sight I ever saw was a lady sitting in the Booking Office. She had a long, very white face and an aquiline nose. Her embroidered dress reached to the ground and, on her head, she wore a high conical hat. She looked like an illustration from a fifteenth century book of hours. It was Edith Sitwell, returning to London after staying with her brother, Sacheverell, at Weston by Weedon.

But a change was coming. Mr Smith retired to a bungalow in Essex. His successors, the Welshman, Oswald Davis and Leslie Battersby from Chester were good men who tried to maintain the old high standards, but the trends were against them. Car ownership was growing and - to make matters worse - the line was transferred from the Eastern to the London Midland Region. The Midland line from St Pancreas served many of the same towns as the Great Central, which, from a 'Midland' perspective seemed an unwanted rival, surplus to requirements. The elegant Gresley Pacifics disappeared to be replaced by 'clapped out' Stainer 5s and Standards, services were reduced, the smaller stations on the line closed and, inevitably, traffic declined further. The Great Central and the Top Station with it were a sitting target for 'the beeching axe'. My father was saddened by it all, but he knew there was nothing that could be done. He got another job and enjoyed a long retirement but part of him was always 'The Booking Clerk at the Top Station'.

John Clarke

GUIDING IN BRACKLEY

Guiding in Brackley started with the registration of the 1st Brackley Guides in approximately 1920, although there had been guiding at Culworth since 1915.

In 1928 the Brackley W.I. and Guides together raised enough money to build a combined headquarters in Manor Road, the Commissioner at that time was Miss Manningham Buller. Most of the original Guides have now passed on but many people will remember Miss Noella Jarvis from Manor Road and Mrs North from Bridge Street who were in the original company.

Guiding was very strong in the sixties and a second company was formed and two more Brownie Packs opened.

Later a third company was formed.

At one time there were more Queens Guides in Brackley than in any other part of the county.

There was always a strong emphasis on camping and the outdoors.

A very active Ranger group was formed in the seventies, this unit received C.H.Q. recognition which was quite a rare distinction.

Guiding continues in Brackley though only one guide company now, the original 1st Brackley; there are three Brownie Packs and two Rainbow units active in the town.

Camping continues to be popular with the girls.

Rosemary Miles.

CHILDHOOD REMINISCENCES OF THE WAR IN BRACKLEY

All the metal railings were taken from the walls in front of the houses, particularly along Oddfellows Terrace (121 - 139 High Street) and up Halse Road. They were given as part of 'the war effort'.

Large quantities of sand were delivered and dumped on the grass bank opposite Oddfellows Terrace and young people helped in the construction of sandbags.

The four principal entries to Brackley were guarded by soldiers who were protected in part by our home-made sandbags. The signposts were of course removed to confuse the enemy.

My mother was designated an air raid warden, and training on what to do in such circumstances was given every Tuesday night at the fire station, so I had to look after my younger brother. The bell at the fire station was tested every Tuesday at 1.00 PM.

I was a pupil at Brackley High School and our new extension was under way. It was to be our hall and gymnasium and remains the gym today at Southfield School. The shower rooms were constructed underneath to a specification that meant they could be used as an air-raid shelter by the pupils in the event of an attack.

I think we were very fortunate in many respects, principally of course in that we were a relatively long way away from any major bombing, although we could see Coventry burning in the night sky. We were touched much less in the countryside by the effects of war although we did have the usual influx of children billeted for their own safety from London and of land girls from Birmingham and similar places. However, there was a greater opportunity to obtain fresh produce, over and above the ration, and - dare I say it - the odd bit of bartering did go on. And there was always the treat of a fresh tomato because Thorpe's (fruitier and florist in the Market Place where Taylor's now is) had their own greenhouses along the Banbury Road.

Our young men went away to war. The territorials were the first to go: the Northamptonshire Yeomanry used to meet at the Drill Hall in St Peter's Road, now Yeoman's Close. But because there were so many airfields round about - Hinton, Turweston and Whitfield to name but three - we had an influx of servicemen, so we had other towns' young men instead.

The YMCA was situated where W J Franklin, the undertaker's is now. After we left school a group of us would go along there to help out on a Sunday evening. The soldiers coming back from weekend leave used to call in. We had to mince Spam, and mix it with baked beans to make it go further, for a sandwich filling. It looked ghastly!

We managed; we pulled together as did people everywhere. We were children and in many ways it was a bit of an adventure and a bit of a fairy story. Much of it seemed so far away, but the names on the War Memorial are testament that Brackley was touched just as every other town, village and city was also.

Suzanne Billingham.

EVENLEY HALL

Northamptonshire has been said to be the country of Spires and Squires and in the southern corner of this shire, the village of Evenley has been able to boast both over the past years.

The spire of St. George's Church stands at the edge of the village whilst the Manor House known as Evenley Hall is situated on the hill between the village and the market town of Brackley.

Evenley Hall has looked across to the village and over the town of Brackley for two hundred and fifty years and presents a pleasing sight across the parkland when travelling southwards on the Brackley By-pass.

It was a gentleman from Cornwall who travelled up to this area in about 1740 to build the manor house in this position. he was a son of the Bassett family who lived in a similar property at Tehidy Park near Camborne. The place is still there but is now a hospital complex for the Cornwall Area Health Authority. However, on a nearby hill stands the Bassett monument, a reminder of former times and family interest.

Francis Bassett's building of Evenley Hall is recorded in Bakers History of Northamptonshire but little else is known as the hall was almost totally demolished by fire in 1897. After Francis Bassett, came several different owners the most notable being Georgina Pierrepont who married the 5th son of Earl Manvers from Thoresby Hall in Nottinghamshire. She was the benefactor for the rebuilding of St. George's church in Evenley which also suffered from a fire. A memorial window to her as well as one for the next owner Col. Campbell are both to be seen in the church.

The last family to be resident was the Allen family. William Henry Allen and his wife Ellen Moulson took up residence in 1890 but had the difficult task of rebuilding the hall after the fire. A excellent job was done by the builders and folk in Brackley still remember their grandparents being involved. A note about the fire in 1897 recalls that it took place at Christmas time and the temperature was so low that the water froze. According to Capt. Norris, the fire tender from Steane Park was sent but to no avail and the building was severally damaged. William Allen's niece remembers being called by her nurse to the window of Brackley house, where she lived, in order to see Evenley Hall on fire. She recalled that she was just two years old at the time.

Things must have quietened down after that and the country life of squire and village settled down to the well ordered system of those days. William Henry and his son, Major Allen who followed him were remembered by the village for the water supply, electricity and the cricket team. The Allens had their own cricket pitch at the top of the parkland.

The end of the era was in sight however and in 1936 the Major died and was buried in Evenley Churchyard. It was then decided that the whole estate, a few farms, fields and houses together with Evenley Hall and the parkland, should be sold off at auction.

The sale took place in 1938 and many villages took the opportunity of purchasing their own property.

It was at that point in time that a business man Frederick Newman Kidd, from Dartford in Kent, who owned a brewery, was looking for a country retreat, particularly as the shadow of war was looming. Evenley Hall fitted his requirements and so he and his family moved there just before the outbreaks of World War II. His daughter, Bobbie, who was about twelve years old then, returned to visit the hall in 1997 and spoke about that time. She said that they had only been there for about six months when the army arrived and asking them to leave at the end of the week. So they left and went to Bournemouth, never to return, and the East Yorks Yeomanry took their place. The army added some extra buildings and along the drive built hard standing plots for the parking of army vehicles. The raised parts on the drive can still be clearly seen. They stayed until D Day in June 1944. They were then however followed for a brief period by evacuees from London where the flying bombs and V2s were causing much concern.

The Kidd family did not go out of the picture because in 1941, Mr Kidd heard Lord Stamp give an appeal on the radio on behalf of the National Children's Home, for property or other gifts to help expand their work of childcare in the country. The National Children's' Home, now called NCH Action for Children, was a

Methodist children's charity, founded by a Methodist Minister, Rev. Thomas Bowman Stephenson in 1869.

Frederick Kidd responded to this appeal most generously by offering Evenley Hall and Parkland to the NCH and this offer was gladly accepted and very much appreciated. A sad story concerning the appeal was that only five days after making the appeal, Lord Stamp was killed by enemy action in London.

It was therefore in 1947 that a new phase in the story of Evenley Hall commenced. Mr William T. Clark came up from South Wales to set up a home for children and very soon the hall and its grounds echoed to the sounds of children enjoying the delights of a place where space was free for all kinds of activity.

Mr Clark, known as Bill to his friends, soon had established the care programme for these children, who through no fault of their own had to live away from their families. The caring was in the form of family groups where up to twelve children, boys and girls, lived together being cared for by a sister of the NCH, specially trained at the NCH training college in London. These women were dedicated workers who had given their life to these children.

When one new youngster asked one of the sisters while she was putting him to bed, 'Who will get me up?' she replied 'I puts thee to bed and I gets thee up.' Life for all was quite tough and Bill kept a firm but caring eye on all the proceedings. When some of the old boys and girls return at their reunions, the tales of old grow more interesting with age. It is usually about recounting their exploits whilst trying to avoid Bill's wary eye when they were up to no good. Swimming was a favourite past-time, not in the clean heated indoor pool of today but in a wide and deeper part of the River Ouse which flowed at the bottom of the park.

They also took part in Scouts and Girls Brigade, country dancing and music. Groups gave performances all over the country at NCH Festivals. This was all apart from the school activities, as they all attended local schools. Often they topped the league in sports as not only did the lads play football very well but a tennis court in the grounds gave them a head start in that game. In 1969 NCH celebrated its centenary and the Evenley hall five a-side football team won the cup against many other branches of the NCH.

The Evenley Hall choir also featured on the BBC Songs of Praise at Manchester Cathedral that year. Another high-light was when the television cameras covered a Christmas party at the hall.

It was of course not all fun and games. Sadness was not far away when one considered that most of the children would have given anything to be in a normal loving family home of their own. But even so, there was the knowledge that if this could not be so, then Evenley Hall was an excellent second place. Like most things in this world, changes were not far away and life at the hall met this when Bill was moved into an area responsibility in 1970 for his final three years before retirement.

Mike Barlow with his wife Ceinwen and four children arrived on the scene to take up residence in the lodge at the end of the Evenley Hall, Lime Tree Drive. This had become the manager's home and it was a very convenient place to note the comings and goings of the hall. This was somewhat different from the days when the chief gardener lived there and had to report to the big house the names of any visitors so that the squire could be prepared.

It was however, still a time of change nationally and in line with general caring policies the number of children was reduced to thirty from the high point of fifty-seven. Staffing now included married couples where the men were expected to take on outdoor activities as well as helping with the care tasks.

The summer holidays were no longer major undertakings of children and staff descending on to a sea-side church, using their premises for sleeping and eating. Catering flats or caravans were taken over by the individual family groups and this gave everyone a greater freedom of choice. It was still possible for a group of older children to take part in canoeing or youth hostelling and during most summers, canoes were part of a Saturday outing to the nearby Oxford Canal. A particular exciting time was when the older children went youth hostelling in winter, particularly when the Christmas holidays from school had been extended to three weeks. These trips usually took in a channel crossing and at times this could be quite rough. Overnight accommodation was usually in a French Youth Hostel or a small guest house. The ferry companies were very well disposed to our request for special consideration regarding costs and the boats generally had few passengers. It was therefore possible for the youngsters to get a glimpse of French life and customs and the ports of Dunkirk, Calais, Boulogne, Le Havre and St. Malo were visited over the years. Le Havre proved to be very exciting as overnight the rain which had fallen froze solidly on the streets and pavements. In the morning it was great fun helping to push the French motorists up the slopes whilst each youngster was trying to keep his or her feet on the ground.

It had also been one of the heavier snowfalls in England that winter and so as we travelled back to Southampton overnight, we found most of the roads snowbound. However, as we had all day to travel and there were some strong lads on board, we set off northwards in our minibus and steadily followed the single track through the snow on the A34 to Oxford where the AA man could not believe that we had come through. A few hours after returning safely home to the hall, more snow fell and the Evenley Hall drive was blocked for several days.

The children still attended the local schools and generally were quite a significant bunch. It was good to hear from one member of staff who organised school walking and camping expeditions on the Ridgeway who said that it was always good to have some Evenley Hall folk around as they knew how to put up tents properly.

Another staff member who had one of the more difficult lads in class, said that his feelings about him changed when he watched him from a distance at the Evenley Fishing ponds. The lad was showing a group of young fisherfolk how to set up their rods and tackle and was letting them know the best place to fish. The staff member could not believe he was such a caring lad.

Back at the hall, there was space. Children who had been deprived of their homes found real freedom in the grounds. There were lawns to play on, woods to keep as nature reserves and trees to climb. Quite often one would hear a voice calling and on looking up you would see a young lad perched forty feet or so up, and it was at such times that an instant prayer was very necessary. One lad even chose to sleep in one of the trees all night.

When the end of schooling was reached and sometimes before, plans would have been worked upon in order that the children could return to their home area and find suitable openings for employment or further education. This was quite a difficult move even though most of the young people were eagerly looking forward to it. In later years, at the reunions, some of them have spoken about the difficulties of readjustment to what might be called an ordinary lifestyle.

It was with this particular difficulty in mind that the social services decided to cease sending children to places such as Evenley Hall. It is always difficult to know whether or not this was a good move, but the change did come and in the early 80s, the end was announced at Evenley Hall. Many there thought that this would be the end of the Hall's role as a caring concern. However, there came another request from the social services. Would the NCH consider offering a residential and day service for young people who had a learning disability, and had left school?

This was quite a challenge but after visiting many different establishments who had been working in this field, the decisions was taken to go ahead. In 1984 seven students, as they were called, arrived to take up a place at the Evenley Hall Community Project. This was so they could take part in a 'Training for Life' programme.

The parents of these seven met together and agreed that the programme was ideal for their dependants and gave it their wholehearted backing. Staff took part in retraining programmes and gradually this day service built up a whole range of skill encouraging activities. The students were given a choice of activity and encouraged to try new skills to enable as much independence to be gained as possible.

Work was also started on the building to convert the children's rooms into student bed-sits and by 1987 there was accommodation for ten students in the main house, four places in a flat and four places in the detached house which had been staff accommodation. There were also places available for anyone who wished to have a short stay.

The training programmes steadily evolved and by 1997, many of the students were able to do some form of 'out work' and attend evening classes in Brackley. They were also able to travel to Banbury College for day courses. Students were encouraged to use public transport where appropriate although the two minibuses and estate car were widely used to enable all this to happen. Day students were collected from home and the journey times kept to a minimum.

This was a great improvement from the days when they had to sit for long periods travelling through the villages to the centres in Northampton.

Independence training, to Training for Life, as the project was called, included holidays and many other outings to places of interest. Students would chose a holiday from a wide range including, hotels, holiday parks, canal cruising and adventure centres. These were great occasions and the staff involved found them to be a most rewarding part of the work.

The supporters of the work, the Friends of Evenley Hall, were a tremendous asset to all. Some volunteers came regularly each week to provide essential extra hands to share the skill making tasks and it was well known that all them found it to be rewarding time.

It was however now apparent to the executive committee of NCH Action for Children that this project of their organisation was moving out of the age range for its charitable status. It therefore became necessary for them to enter into discussion with the social services to look for another charity to take over the work.

After about two years of planning and decision taking, from a short list of organisations, the Shaftesbury Society was chosen to manage the project, and this commenced in January 1997.

The Hall and its parkland still belonged to NCH Action for Children and it was the plan for the property to be sold and the income put back into childcare. Meanwhile the Shaftesbury Society was given a five year lease of the hall to continue the work and plan for the future.

At present, in 1999, this plan concerns a move for everyone at the hall to transfer into smaller accommodation in Brackley with the day work continuing in a similar form but also in Brackley premises.

The future occupation of Evenley Hall is therefore once again uncertain and the hope can only be that in the new millennium, whoever occupies the place will ensure that the traditions of Evenley Hall will not be forgotten. The potential for a continued caring regime is quite considerable and as in 1941 it might be that one well disposed benefactor will come along and give hope to many as Mr Kidd did at that time.

Michael Barlow.

A POEM FROM THE PAST

THE WOMEN'S INSTITUTE
OR HOWLS OF A HUSBAND

Oh! Where, and oh! Where! Is my good wife gone tonight?
Why! She's gone to Women's Institute, and I ask you! Is it right?
That she should go out once a month, and leave me all alone!
For it will be two weary hours before she does come home!
So now I've put the kids to bed, and got some time to spare,
I'll tell you about the W.I. and things that they do there -
They make nice woolly hearthrugs and put new seats in chairs,
They've even learnt to cure the skins of rabbits, sheep and hares -
They cover old umbrellas, if holes in them you've tore
But what's the use of doing that if it ain't going to rain no more?
At Christmas time they ice the cakes, make gifts and lollipops,
And of course they're all much better, than you can buy in shops!
They learn to mend the pots and pans, and jobs of gardening too -
In fact, there'll soon be nothing left, for us poor chaps to do!
I've heard it whispered lately, that Brackley folks are slow!
That's not true of the women for they're always on the go -
They tell me now they're going to build a fine big roomy hall,
'Cause they haven't got one large enough to hold 'em nearly all,
So in another month or two, I'll bet you my last bob
They'll have got the bricks and mortar, and started on the job,
My wife's made me some slippers she can even mend a boot!
And next, I fear she'll try her hand, at making me a suit -
Of course I shall have to wear it, or she'll say 'ungrateful brute!'

Let's hope they'll learn to make 'em fit, at the Women's Institute.

G.C.
June 1928.

DID YOU KNOW...?

In the 17th century there were twenty-seven pubs and an ale house in the main street of Brackley.

King George VI and Queen Elizabeth alighted at the Bottom Station in 1950 on the Royal visit to Silverstone. The station was wonderfully spruced up for the occasion, but at the last moment a fish box had to provide a necessary step down from the train!

The Fire Brigade stabled its two horses at the Crown hotel till 1932.

The Feoffee Charity, dates from 1608 and since then has given money each year to the church, the schools, and the poor, though it has certainly moved on from the 4d given to each of the twenty-four widows every Good Friday in the 17th century.

There is Morris Dancing every May morning in Brackley - a long held tradition. There is even a Brackley tune. Morris Dancing originated from the Moors in Spain and was brought to England by the Crusaders on their way home.

Brackley was the first small town in the county to twin with a French town, and the first small town in the county to twin also with a German town. Twinning began in the early 70s and is flourishing still.

The Parish Magazine of 1884 records the offertory in May totalled 1,548 coins. (£2.15.9 3/4). There were five burials in May - these persons were aged 39, 58, 31 and 54 years and 12 hours.

In 1963 there were no new houses in Brackley, and there was not one house for sale.

Mary Yates.

BRACKLEY INFANT SCHOOL

In September 1951 my husband and I came to live in Brackley with my two step-children, Antony 16 and Rosalind 12. I had never lived in the countryside before so I had a lot to learn.

Brackley was a delightful little town with a population of about three and a half thousand. The Borough Council had been building a large number of council houses. Westhill Avenue and Beaumont Crescent were just about completed and Waynflete Avenue still needed a lot more building done. The town was surrounded by farmland. From our rear windows all we could see were fields, trees, hedgerows and every so often, down in the cutting, a train could be heard either going to Banbury or to Bletchley. There was the Bottom Station near where we now have a Police Station.

I assured my husband that when we moved here, there was sure to be a school which needed a teacher in their infant department, so I made some enquiries. Yes, there was an infant school. It had three classes, one for each of the three years as an infant and no, there were no vacancies.

In January, I managed to find a post at Neithrop Infant School in Banbury. I caught the 8.10 bus each morning at 9p - old pennies - each way, and a second bus from the town centre up to Neithrop where I had a class in a temporary building. The children were in their second year at school and we got along very well. In the September they moved into the main school and were in the top class. I was given the job of being with them for another three terms.

As a result we bonded to such an extent that we were all very sad to have to part at the end of the school year when they went up to the junior school. We hugged each other and some of us cried. It was like losing a family.

After a final term I heard that there was to be a vacancy at the Brackley Infant School in the reception class, my favourite age group.

I only heard about it by pure chance. Whilst I was going out of the town every day I knew no one at all, but a group of people decided that the town could do with a Dramatic Society, so they put leaflets around inviting people to come to the first meeting. The result was a Dramatic Society. BADS was formed. To begin with they were suspicious of me when I told them I had lived in Brackley for two years as they had never seen me in the town and in those days if two local people were chatting in the Market Place and a face they didn't recognise went by it was so unusual they would say to each other, 'Who's that?' 'Never seen them before!'

One of the members of BADS was the head of the Infant School and in the autumn of 1953 she asked me if I would like to take over a class as the teacher was leaving at the end of the autumn term.

I was allowed to leave Neithrop without the usual term's notice, so in January 1954 I began what was to be an over twenty-five years' life working with the local children when they first started school, the reception class.

I was in for a shock. The buildings are still there. at the corner of High Street and Hill Street. To the rear is a small brick building with two rooms, which in '54 were classrooms. The smaller room was for the five year olds, forty-eight of them, squeezed in so tightly that any child who walked down the small gap between the desks and the wall, dislodged any picture put up there. It was all very old and grubby. All the woodwork, even the handle of the little spade in the tiny sand tray, was riddled with woodworm.

There were two ancient desks to seat five at the back of the room which had the seat attached to the desk by heavy iron work. When one of the five children in either desk wanted to get out, the others had to move out as well to make it possible. The rest of the furniture was a mixed lot of tables and small chairs. The walls were brickwork with a cover of distemper. It had probably been the same for years.

The war had been over for eight years, but there were still a lot of shortages and paper for the children to use was in very short supply. I filled the gap by bringing in duplicate copies from my husband's order books to use the blank reverse side.

The pencils the children were expected to use were the small ends, well-chewed, handed down from the top class. I had a desk and chair with a tall cupboard behind me. To open it I had to get off my chair, which was pressed against the cupboard and push the chair under the table. The contents of the cupboard were some very old reading books called 'Old Lob'. I made quite a large quantity of reading matter for the children and used an ancient worm holed blackboard and easel, but I had to be alert as the easel was up against the door between my class and the top class next door and if the head teacher came through the door, the blackboard fell on my head if I didn't move in time.

In spite of all the short comings and difficulties, we had a happy time together and most of the children were much nicer than city and big town children.

There was little in the way of equipment. The only items in the P.E. box were some ancient 'sorbo' balls with bits of the sponge middle missing and a few frayed skipping ropes. I found the caretaker's ladder across the tops of the four lavatory cubicles in the small building in the middle of the playground. I found that if I tied it to the railings between the infant and junior playgrounds, they could climb up it from the bottom end on the ground to the top where they slipped between the rungs and dropped about nine inches to the ground: the nearest we could get to an adventure playground.

At the end of the school year, all my class moved up to Mrs Thomas, the teacher of the six year olds. Her classroom was in the junior school and she had fifty children to teach. So had the headteacher, Miss Jarvis in the classroom next to mine.

The town continued to grow and more and more children were needing a school place, so the county education authority hired a large room on the other side of Hill Street. It was the Methodist Sunday School. There was also a kitchen and at the rear of the building, an adult lavatory, reached by a path right round the building. A trench was dug out for the boys' urinal. There was a stone wall all round the building so as long as I secured the wooden gates with a skipping rope, the children were safe. Yes, we moved out of our tiny room to a huge room with an ancient piano and two brand new coke-devouring heaters, one at each end of the room.

There was one cupboard for our use. After my two years in a very small room, I was delighted and so were the children. There was a downside. We were completely isolated from the rest of the school except for playtimes when I had to see my children across the dangerous little street and then back again.

When in September, my children moved up to the class above, it was, for them, like starting school all over again.

The old five seater desks were due to be disposed of , so I asked if I could have the five foot long seats which were lovely solid wood, polished to a high standard by generations of fidgety bottoms. One was made into a sea-saw by a kind American dad and the other I made into a slide.

At last we had room to do all sorts of things that were impossible in the tiny room we had left.

I made a lot of work-related pictures and charts, but the children who came to Sunday School tended to spoil them, so they were mounted on cardboard and removed from the walls at the end of Friday afternoon, and put away until Monday morning.

I took a wireless up to the schoolroom and we would sit and enjoy 'Listen With Mother' in the afternoon. I was able to play the ancient piano for singing games. The four years I spent there were very happy ones.

Then, in 1960, a new infant school with four classrooms was built in Waynflete Avenue and, in the September we all moved there on the land next door to the Secondary Modern School.

We moved out of the Victorian age into the twentieth century. We were given new tables and chairs; we were allowed for the first time to choose what we would like to have in our classrooms, books, plenty of paper, paint and easels, P.E. apparatus and a splendid piano. Oh! So many things that made every day seem like a birthday. There was a huge hall with two classrooms at each end, a cloakroom for each class and boys and girls toilets with HOT water in the four miniature washbasins.

We settled in very happily, but the number of children was steadily rising as the town grew and the school had two new classrooms built on at the rear in 1968. We were now a six class school.

The children left the infant school when they were seven and moved up to the junior school which was still in the High Street and they had to work hard to be ready to pass the dreaded 11+ in order to go to the boys' Magdalen College School in the Market Square or the Brackley Girls High School in Banbury Road. Both schools had some children who were boarders and the schools were staffed by some well remembered personalities.

When comprehensive education took over in the early 70s, Magdalen became one of the two sites for both girls and boys the other site was the Secondary Modern School which became known as the Waynflete Site.

The Girls School was to change completely and was altered by builders and other workmen to become a new school known as Southfield Primary School and gradually grew to become the biggest primary in the county.

There was a private school known as St John's School, in Banbury Road. It was well thought of in the town and one of its former pupils speaks highly of its standard of education.

She is Caryl Billingham who is, now, for the third time Town Mayor of Brackley. She speaks well of the Girls High School and she went on to further education and, in her 20s, became one of the three directors at a famous local firm producing contact lenses which has a world-wide market: a good example of local education.

The town continued to grow. By 1968 a new junior school was built at the top end of Manor Road as more and more children needed school places; we were introduced to mobile classrooms. They were far from ideal as the children had to go out in the open for P.E., for morning assembly, or for loos and handwashing. Even if it was pouring with rain or there was deep snow, it was the only way.

By 1985, it was obvious that there must be a new primary school built so plans were made and approved by the education committee at County Hall and Brackenleas Primary School was built at the top end of Pavilions Way. In the last two years more classrooms have been built on in order to take in the ever-increasing number of children.

I wish that the town didn't have to grow any larger, but am afraid that it will. Bigger definitely isn't better.

I have enjoyed living and teaching in the same town as I could see my children grow up. One of them, Geoffrey Wilkins, was

Town Mayor in 1986 and I, as a fellow Town Councillor, proposed him for the position. At his Mayor - making ceremony he called me up to the platform and presented me with a gilt carrige-clock. On the top was the inscription 'To Mrs Thorpe with sincere thanks from the children of Brackley'. Well, I could say 'Thank you' to all of my past little friends. You gave me the happiest twenty-five years of my life.

    Bless you.

Tilly Thorpe.

MAGDALEN MEMORIES

I first came to M.C.S. Brackley in January 1946 just after the end of World War II, just like my uncle HWP had done after World War I over twenty years before me. I came into the second term of the School Certificate year from a Choir School in Cambridge and struggled, not surprisingly, with all subjects except Mathematics and Latin which had been my staple academic diet previously.

I soon settled and made friends living in 'The Lodgings' (later Magdalen House) where the Rev. Arthur and Mrs Bolton were in charge. Memories of so long ago are mostly about members of staff; some are affectionate memories, others more amusing. Some strange people took up teaching just after the war.

First of all then: dear old Mr Blencowe (FAB) the music master; organist of numerous churches in the Brackley area. He gave me my first organ lessons in the school chapel, just as he had my uncle Howard back in the twenties. A kind man, rather fussy, a bit like a dear old lady in the nicest sort of way. He dyed his hair, or at least part of it, with henna! Sadly, he only taught me for a short while, because he died in February 1947. I then had to start playing the organ for the school's Sunday service. After a time, Mr Morrish came to teach music. He had very poor eyesight. The boys were rather cruel to him. During singing lessons they would gently push the piano so that he had to move the stool back a few inches; this continued until he was trapped in the corner of the room. Other boys would ask to be 'excused'; go out, then climb back through the window, unnoticed, and ask to be 'excused' again. 'But you've just been', said Mr Morrish. 'No that was last week' said the intrepid boy. Mr Morrish wondered if his memory was playing tricks. Control of a class was not his forte.

Next comes to mind Freddie Grunder: a teacher of French of Swiss extraction. On Sundays, the duty master had to read the lessons in chapel. Freddie practised carefully, then came out one Sunday in his inimitable mid-European accent with: 'Here beginness the third chapter of the book of the prophet Exodus...'. Poor Bill Bolton, the master, nearly had apoplexy.

Then there was Captain Brooks who ran the Cadet Corps: bow-legged with a twitch and a vaguely American accent. The Corps never lacked equipment. Capt. Brooks would go out with a gang of boys and return with lorry loads of stores from the nearby army camps. I have no idea whether these items were surplus stores or whether the Quartermaster was bribed, but I have my suspicions.... Shooting with a 0.22 rifle was fun and we won many competitions; some targets were shot by the boys, other had the 'bull' blasted out at point blank range I expect. We were awarded a shield for our 100% pass rate. It was all a fiddle. Each inspecting sergeant had been bribed to tell the cadets the questions they were going to get in the next test. We were quick learners. Captain Brooks left rather suddenly. Rumour had it that he was an American deserter. Enough said.

Before I get taken to court for libel I must point out that there were plenty of good teachers who were more normal sorts of people with only a few idiosyncrasies.

E.T. (Daddy) Green, sometimes known as 'spring heeled Jack' because of his bouncy walk.

The Rev. Arthur (Bill) Bolton:- During a fire practice: 'Don't throw that rope ladder out like that, you'll break my study window. Do it like this. (He throws)....*Crash, tinkle, tinkle.*' He was a better shot with a cane.

Mrs Bolton who taught Chemistry from her own text book. Quote: 'Johnny finding life a bore, drank some H_2SO_4 ; Johnny's father, an MD gave him $CaCO_3$; now he's neutralised, it's true; but he's full of CO_2.

E.N.(Ned) Jones. Walked like a chicken. Brilliant Latin master, bridge player and smoker. His mark books were a model of neatness and excellence; they were still available for inspection in 1990. I hope they have not been thrown out.

E.G.(Forrey) Forrester. Could scare the life out of most boys, staff, parents, governors, and all the officials at County Hall. Had a kind heart. Preached a few unprintable sermons! (Send a stamped addressed envelope and a donation for charity for further details).

I could go on about others. I could tell you about the food: Buffalo Monkey Pie etc. I could sneak on a few boys, but they may be still around.

I end by saying that I enjoyed my time at MCS and left in July 1950, marching out at the head of the Corps proudly wearing my War Cert. 'A' badge.... only to return again in 1965 as a member of staff. That is another story.

Why did they call me 'Potty'?

Eddie Palmer.

BRACKLEY FIRE BRIGADE 1906

MEMORIES OF BRACKLEY 1900 - 1999

I first remember the name of Brackley as early as 1941, for I used to travel from Aylesbury to Rugby and Brackley Top Station was the only stop, before my getting off point, Central Station Rugby. Then it was in Easter week of 1951 that we came to live at Elm Tree Farm in the Parish of Evenley and only one mile south of Brackley, with me were my husband Frank, and two small boys three and a half and eighteen months. Brackley was a small market town with a population of three thousand five hundred. Food, stationery and petrol coupons were still in use, so Ration Books had to be re-addressed etc. There was no electricity for the first six weeks, so our paraffin lamps and candles were still needed! On approaching the town from Towcester, it was the buildings and colour of bricks which took my eye: the Almshouses, the lovely Winchester House School, for boarders, The Church of England School, called Feed My Lambs at the corner of Hill Street and still on the right hand side, the lodge which was being used for council offices. Then Brackley House which was a residential home for the elderly, opposite, the Magdalen Chapel and Grammar School caught my eye with their distinctive tall chimneys. In the space which is now a car park, was a cattlemarket, with Monday being market day. A Mr Foot was the auctioneer for Stace and Foot. The Town Hall frontage looked northwards and divided two roads. The chemist, Boots faced the Town Hall. The main hotel The Crown overlooked the Market Place.

As we continued on our way down Bridge Street we had to cross a hump back bridge; this was going over the Bottom Station line, a diesel train ran from Bletchley to Banbury and the line was a single track in places; the driver had to pass over to the signal man a wooden baton. The second bridge we came to was over a tributary of the Ouse, of which Brackley area has two. We were now crossing into Evenley Parish and the road on its way to Oxford was flanked by mature beech trees, making a canopy overhead. On the brow of this hill and opposite Evenley Hall Lodge, was the entrance to Elm Tree Farm, which was a field away from the main road. It was a bungalow farm house with three bedrooms, two receptions, kitchen and bathroom, and was built by a Mr Turner of Brackley. 1946 or 7 it used to be part of the Evenley Hall estate. We had bought 109 acres from a Mr C. Shepherd I was really pleased with the position; and it was to become a settled home. The view from the kitchen window over looked the viaduct in the distance, the very one I crossed ten years before!

We started farming with a small milking herd, as this brought in a monthly cheque so there were stands for twelve cows, and a petrol engine to operate the milking buckets, and the suction teats were carefully put on to the udders of the cows.

This bucket was really heavy and had to be lifted up to the container which cooled the milk before running into a churn.

The churns were then taken to the end of the drive and placed on a platform for the milk lorry to pick up. He then left empty churns for the next day. All these milking implements then had to be washed well in *cold* water - in the outside dairy. We also kept sheep - which when ready for market in the autumn were walked down the main road to Brackley Market, and penned up - This I think was quite an achievement; all hands were needed to get them there safely. The arable fields needed early attention and ground had to be prepared for sowing. We had a contractor come with his combine, and bag the corn up as he went along the field. When the bag was tied up it was put on a chute and so dropped on the ground! These of course all had to be picked up by hand and brought into the buildings. Sometimes if the corn was dry and the price was right it could be sold from the field.

The next year we were able to start breeding lambs in the spring. This was a job that could not be neglected, going out in all weathers last thing with a torch, as they were outside. All farmers hated rain and frost at this time. Later on the sheep were put indoors and so made this job much easier and kinder for the animals.

Sheep shearing was another job in May and this was a real back aching job and needed good weather as the wool had to be dry. This job was done using a hand machine which had to be tuned at a certain speed and evenness.

Ration books and petrol coupons were still required, so I was pleased to find the shops provided all our needs. The butcher and baker came twice a week to the out lying farms and villages and a postman by 7.30 am on his bike!

Now the farm looks out over Tesco's - so times have certainly changed.

Jane Snell.

A POEM FROM THE PAST

BRACKLEY

Oh! Blest are those people, whose fortunate lot
Is to dwell in old Brackley - that beautiful spot,
The High Street's an avenue - splendid old trees,
With seats where we old folk can rest if we please -
And we gaze on the old Chapel Tower and our mind
Must dwell on the past: Ah! Then we were blind
To the beauties around us, and little we'd care
As long as we'd sixpence to spend at the Fair;
But there's rumours abroad, that a change is in sight,
And we dream that queer buildings spring up in the night
'Factories! A cinema! No, no!' says old John
'Give me my fireside, and let well alone!'
'We've a Brewery here where they brew some good ale,
From a well which they say is ne'er known to fail,
So drought does not frighten us, floods pass us by
For the bright town of Brackley stands well, high and dry.'
'Bright town indeed!' cries young Jack in disgust
'If it don't soon get brighter, well! Leave it I must!'
So let's have some factories! A cinema too!
WHAT! Who's going to build them?
                                    I DON'T KNOW! DO YOU?

G.C.
March 1937.

CHARTER CELEBRATIONS
700TH ANNIVERSARY

I was Mayor of Brackley (1959-60) and Chairman of the Septcentenary Planning Committee. It was therefore my sole responsibility to plan and to implement a programme that was a suitable celebration of this historic event.

We felt that royalty should be present, and I felt that the bestowal of the Freedom of the Borough on the Northamptonshire Yeomanry would be the necessary spur to have the Duke and Duchess of Gloucester present at the ceremony.

Protocol demands that the invitation and all the arrangements should be in the hands of the Lord Lieutenant, Earl Spencer, (the father of the Lord Spencer who was Princess Diana's father). With some trepidation I drove to Althorp to see the Earl. I told him who I was, and of our intention of offering the freedom to the Yeomanry. What I did not know was that it was Earl Spencer's Grandfather who formed the Yeomanry in the first place. So he was very happy to help me, but he would himself have a word with the Duke of Gloucester. However I would have to send an official invitation and liaise with the equerries at St. James' Palace over details. That was done, and in due course I got an affirmative reply from the Duke's office.

Earl Spencer then wanted to meet Betty, as she would be sitting next to the Duke, to see that she would be suitable! I need not have worried; he was very impressed and being Chairman of Northampton Bench, a few weeks later he asked Betty to become a magistrate.

There were lots more practical details to sort out. A civic luncheon for two hundred people; this would be held in the lower Town Hall, as there were cooking facilities there. It was time for the first committee meeting, as we needed careful planning and support. The royal visit concentrated everyone's minds. The response was heart-warming; there was no dissension. A well-known firm of caterers were to provide the lunch. Bromley's gave a wonderful presentation box of soap to every guest. We tried to include a representative of every aspect of Brackley life, and notable citizens;

all very difficult to know where to draw the line. But the ceremony was still three months off and we had to find all the Yeomen and a band. Earl Spencer found a band of the Life Guards for us, and Yeomen appeared from all over the place, about three hundred of them; all very anxious to come on parade.

At the same time the committee were coming out with lots of ideas of what could be done to fill up the fortnight's celebrations. There was to be a carnival and ox roast, an agricultural show with horse jumping, and cattle and sheep. There was an old time dance and the Dramatic Society put on 'Queen Elizabeth' a historical pageant. The British Legion went on parade. The USAAF at Croughton supplied all the loud speaker systems. There was no organisation in the town that was not fully committed, and with no apparent fuss. Mind you I was a very strict Chairman, and anyone straying from the point under discussion was reminded of it! Even so it was all very friendly, and no one took offence.

Saturday, May 21st was rapidly approaching. I had to make three very important speeches. These were prepared and everything was set for the great day. The luncheon in the Town Hall was at 12.30 pm. At 2pm was the march past of the Northamptonshire Yeomanry headed by the Life Guard Band. I made a general proclamation from the centre of the parade ground (there was no car park in the Market Square then), and presented to the officer commanding an illuminated scroll within a cavalry saddle bag, with a gold replica of the Borough Coat of Arms. This scroll gave the formal consent to march through Brackley with 'colours flying, bayonets fixed and bands playing'. I then had to inspect the troops. The band played a slow march, and I was very glad I had been taught how to slow march at school in the O.T.C. Apparently it was very impressive.

Colin Miller.

DANCE IN BRACKLEY
1943 - 2000

My family moved to Brackley in war years, 1943, when my father took the headship of the Secondary Modern School (now the Waynflete site of M.C.S.) His name was William Edward Taylor.

Sister Monica was then age twenty and I was twelve and we had trained in the world of dance ever since I was two and a half in Kent, London and in Nottingham and Bristol.

We lived, at first in a big house, then, the vicarage, in the High Street as there wasn't a house for us, but later in 1945 we moved to 73 Halse Road.

I attended Brackley High School and my sister started ballet and dance classes in Brackley, originally at The Bell Tower. She was always a pioneer with her teaching and thousands must have passed through her hands, enjoying her teachings and guidance. I was one of them.

Over the decades we must have raised quite a lot of funds and supported no end of local events and charities - displays, shows, festivals and fêtes.

My sister's 'right hand' was my Mother Marjoire, who was not only a wonderful mother but made every stitch we ever wore; every costume we ever danced in and for me, later in professional theatre. She took a pride in it, loved it.

Monica entered many of her pupils for the Banbury Arts and Crafts Festival each year. I, again took part in the first two.

At age sixteen I was the first girl in Northants to be awarded a County Grant for training in ballet and the theatre arts. So my life was out of the area for many years, training in London and then a wide and varied career followed: in ballet company, musicals, TV and West End cabaret. I was in the famous musical 'Oklahoma!' on a long tour of two and a half years. Many local friends came to see me when we played theatres in Northampton or Oxford, and we were the first musical ever to play the Stratford-on-Avon Theatre (then the Shakespeare Memorial Theatre) in 1953. Quite an experience!

Monica continued to teach in Brackley, Buckingham and Bicester for many years.

In 1962 I started a teaching career, first with a small school in Warwick and then five years with a big well known London ballet school.

In 1982 I choreographed 'West Side Story' for Magdalen College and later also 'The Boy Friend', 'Grease' and 'Noah's Fludde'.

Monica became ill in 1994-5 and is now, sadly, in a nursing care home.

Ann Steedman.

BRACKLEY HIGH SCHOOL FOR GIRLS
AS I REMEMBER IT 1930 - 1935

The school was opened in the early twenties or before as I know of two people in their nineties who both attended the school.

I began my school days there in April 1935, a very daunting day for me.

I cycled to Brackley every day in all weathers in the company at that time of four other girls, Beryl Watson, Cissie Humphrey, Margorie Gulliver and Nancy Branson. We had a school uniform for summer and winter. Navy blue gymslips, cream blouses for summer and navy flannel blouses for winter, with green French knots embroidered on the collar, a narrow green tie, black lisle stockings, black outdoor shoes (lace up) and black indoor shoes, and galoshes had to be worn outside in wet weather when crossing the Main Road to Highfield House. There were plimsolls to be worn, two pairs one with black laces for games, green laces for gym. All the shoes were kept in a linen shoe bag hanging in the cloakroom, with the girl's name embroidered on it. All spare stockings and shoes left out of bags were confiscated.

We wore white Panama hats in summer and black velour hats in winter, all with a green and navy striped band and both hats were very difficult to keep on whilst cycling.

Hats always had to be worn with the school uniform. All clothes were purchased from Bradley's shop near the Town Hall. We had very nice navy school blazers, for everyone had a badge with B.H.S. on the breast pockets.

School began with assembly each morning for hymns, prayers and notices, with one of the pupils playing the piano. Miss Kate Whitehead would conduct the ceremony. Also held on Friday afternoons Roman Catholic pupils had their own religious services. The pupils were divided into four houses who all wore badges, Egerton - yellow badges, Grafton - red badges, Stanley - blue badges and Crewe - mauve badges.

Every girl belonged to one of these houses. I was in Egerton. There was a house captain and girls had good points for well marked homework and bad points for misbehaviour e.g. talking in class etc. These were credited or debited to the house. Each house had a plot of garden bordering the drive which had to be cultivated with flowers and kept tidy. Everyone was supposed to help; there was a competition in the summer for the best kept garden, and points were awarded.

The sports day up Manor Road was one of the events of the year when parents were invited. This was on Mr Allen's land where the grass tennis courts were quite a long walk from the High School.

There were hard tennis courts at the school. This was where everyone assembled for their lunch and dinner time breaks to have a chat.

Hockey was played up the Oxford Road, quite a long walk, and later in Mr Watkin's field in Banbury Road, where afterwards cattle grazed.

Swimming was at the open air baths in Buckingham Road, where Cecil Rose was the instructor, another long walk.

Hockey was later transferred to the Council School playing fields in Manor road adjoining the Winchester house playing fields.

Pupils came to the school from a large area, and by various means of transport, buses, trains, cycles etc. The Banbury bus (Midland Red) brought pupils from Banbury, Middleton Cheney, Farthinghoe etc. whilst pupils came on the LNER Great Central Railway from Woodford, Halse, Eyden, Culworth, Helmdon etc. They had a very long walk from the station to the High School. The LMS Railway brought pupils from Winslow, Padbury, Buckingham etc. They walked up Bridge Street.

One pupil had to ride her pony to Brackley and stable it at the Locomotive Inn whilst the ones from Tusmore Park were brought to and fro in a very small pony trap. They were Peggy and Eileen Bell and Joan Bell. How I envied them.

School boarders were housed at Highfield House in Banbury Road. Miss Constance Whitehead, sister to Miss Kate was in charge of their well being. The hall at the Boarding House was used for gym, needlework and music (Mr Arnold Blencoe was the music master for singing etc.) and Miss Bull taught the piano. School lunches were also taken at the school hall, we paid 2/6 per term if you took sandwiches for the use of a plate, and 1/- per day for a hot meal.

Gym was later transferred to the W.I. hall and cookery and needlework transferred to the Council School in Manor Road.

A new uniform was introduced, green gingham dresses for summer and navy pinafore skirts for winter and the narrow green ties were replaced by a green navy and white tie.

Mr Blencoe was the only male teacher in the school, others who I remember were Miss Pringle, Miss Harris, Miss Cook, Miss Roberts and Miss Traneker who is still with us in Brackley. Miss Arnold was the games mistress.

We weren't allowed to go into Brackley during our dinner or lunch break without a special note and definitely no fraternising with the Magdalen College Boys.

Many girls congregated in the bike shed during the lunch break and in wet weather, many pranks and tales were hatched there.

Once a year we had to line up on the tennis court to have a group photo taken, I've still got two of mine the first year I was in the High School and the last. Framed photos of the pupils groups hung in the school corridor approaching form 3B. I wonder what happened to all those photos. On them I would recognise relatives and friends from the time the school opened.

Miss Beatrice Cartwright was one of the school managers and was often seen coming down the drive accompanied by her little dog. She was Mayor of Brackley for a while, and a relative of the Cartwrights of Aynhoe, her nephew Richard Cartwright was one of the school governors. He and his son were tragically killed in a car accident.   School speech days were held either at the Town Hall or W.I. Hall, when all the local dignitaries would assemble on the platform, with the Town Mayor, governors etc, for the prize giving and speeches.

Every Armistice Day November 11th the school had to march to the War Memorial for the Service of Remembrance joined by other schools in the town. Each year the Grafton Hunt met on the Market Square on that day.

We had three subjects of homework each night and five at weekends - there was strict discipline about running around corridors or the quadrangle. Prefects were supposed to keep order and report anyone breaking any rules.

There were more fee paying girls than scholarship pupils and there was a fee paying preparatory school for girls under ten years of age. I used to take my school fee on the first day of term, I forget what sum it was.

For wet weather we had navy gabardine macs, very useful when cycling from Helmdon in all weathers, and wintertime navy great coats and school scarves. Navy, white and green.

Mr Watts was the gardener and handy man. He kept the buildings tidy and attended to the heating arrangements for the whole school.

I am not certain when the High School opened as such. I well remember many girls much older than I attending the school. One is now ninety-five years old and one, ninety-two.

I enjoyed my school days at the High School very much; I only wish I had worked a bit harder there and had achieved something that would benefit me in later days.

Mary Turnham.

ST PETER'S CHURCH

Apart from minor structural changes, St Peter's Church has remained in its original form since 1283 A.D.

In the last four decades there have been two major reordering and reconstruction projects, which helped to retain the building in its original concept.

During the year 1989, the then Bishop of Peterborough, Bishop (Bill) William Westwood issued a challenge to all parishes in the diocese, to offer forward plans to strengthen and allow for growth in the parish. We, at St Peter's were successful in obtaining a grant of two hundred thousand pounds to help us achieve our dream. The eventual project was to cost us nearly four hundred thousand pounds, and in the autumn of 1996 we started the extension, which has given us toilets, kitchen and a multi-purpose hall, designed to be in sympathy with the original building.

At St Peter's we are proud of what we have achieved and are sure we have put the church on a firm footing for the next millennium.

Mike Cassford.

THE CHAPEL OF ST JOHN AND ST JAMES
MAGDALEN COLLEGE SCHOOL BRACKLEY

One of the most beautiful school chapels in England, its history goes back eight hundred years. The chapel has changed hands several times, has sometimes fallen into decay, but been restored again due to the efforts of many good people through the centuries. It was originally attached to a hospital for the poor, which was later sold to Magdalen College, Oxford part of the endowment by William of Waynflete, Bishop of Winchester. It has long been used for worship by the people of Brackley as well as being the school chapel.

One of its finest features is the beautiful East Window.

Mary Yates.

A POEM FROM THE PAST

RHYMING ROUND BRACKLEY

Some people say that Brackley's dull, and this I think is folly
As all the people in it, are mostly gay and jolly -
Advantages we have, no doubt, and those we need not part with,
Peculiarities? Of course! And here's a few to start with -
Our BARNES are never full of corn, and STILES you can't climb
over,
But you may get inside the CROWN, and lunch on Sole from Dover
You cannot buy a cabbage, or brussels sprouts at GREENS
But you may purchase rhubarb (pills) and also (bile) beans.
'Some ADAMS' apples' did you say? My! What a strange request!
You'll get them at the corner shop, the penny ones are best -
Our fishmonger sells PLUMB'S of course, and yet 'tis strange to
say,
If you want a bit of SALMON, you must go across the way! -
And there, next door, I do de-CLARE, are antiques old and musty,
But if you have another look, you'll find they're not so dusty -
A snack bar's rather handy here; - this shows the owner's wit,
He doesn't put his name outside, but just says 'THIS IS IT' -
Our GARDENERS getting rather old and very seldom digs
He much prefers to handle a nice fat bunch of pigs -
Our SHEPHERD never tended sheep, but bought one for a dollar,
He ate the mutton, kept the wool to stuff a horse's collar -
The LOCOMOTIVE never runs along the railway line,
A pint of beer, you may drink here, the local brew is fine -
We've got a GREYHOUND and a FOX, a BIRD that doesn't sing,
Some KEYS that will not unlock doors, and a BELL that will not
ring -
The LION never roars at all, since HOLLAND cut his hair,
At least the barber told me so, last time I 'took the chair' -
A spotted dog sits by the gate, of the ancient Temperance House
Hikers or bikers need not fear, he wouldn't harm a mouse -
St. Peters is a fine old church, the vicar's name is DANTER
He trots on Shank's pony, but he might prefer to canter -

We've MARK and MATTHEWS, SIMONS, JOHN and many
another Saint
And then there's MASTER WILL who'll give your house a lick of
paint -
Another very worthy man has proved himself quite handy,
His legs are straight as scaffold poles, and yet they call him BANDY
'If winter comes' well! What PRYCE SUMMERS! Perhaps you are
aware!
That if he shouldn't be at home, you'll find him 'on the Square' -
'Tis true we have no cinemas and that's a thousand pities,
But our MAYOR and corporation are the envy of the cities -
On Coronation Day you'd see them, marching up the street
With Borough Band a-playing, and MOSS with mace complete -
Our Legionaries would fill a WARD, and BEN WOOD be there too,
If you want a useful basket made, well - he's the man for you!
The PARISH news of course you've read, of how some wicked
sprite
Pulled up our Coronation tree, 'twas late one Saturday night,
No witness was there of the deed, no woman, child NOR - MAN,
A fiver's offered for a 'catch' so earn it if you can -
'What's in a name' you well may ask! And this one's surely VYLE,
But for master's shirts and madam's gowns, you can't beat them for
style -
Does MR HAY - MAN build a rick, or share in farmer's joys?
Oh! No he merely 'raises cane' on naughty little boys! -
Talking of farmers - here I think, 'tis only WRIGHT to say
They don't believe in borrowing the PLOUGH across the way -
We've got two pretty little banks, whereon no wild thyme blows
But if you plant your money there, you'll see how quick it grows!
When neighbour Bertie and his wife, went for a ROW one morning
The BOTTOM of the boat fell out, without the slightest warning!
Poor Bertie spied a passer by, and shouted 'Help! 'oi, 'oi, sir',
'With pleasure friend,' the man replied (his name I think was
BOISSIER) -
But just then, Mr GRAY came up with walking stick in hand sir,
He held his stick out to the pair, and pulled them safe to hand sir,
Some years ago two Scottish lads, came down to Brackley Town

One of them is a SMART-ish chap, the other is no clown,
For he a FORTUNE means to make, and this seems pretty clear
That if he's making 'siller,' it must be out of BEER -
Don't go to SANDALS for your shoes, or Mr PLANK'S for wood;
Their names may be misleading but their bread is very good -
'Once upon a time' 'tis said, a boy from Magdalen School
Just ran home to his Pa and Ma, which was against the rule,
The College dons were in dismay, and kicked up quite a din!
'We'll put a BOLT-ON now,' they said 'and that'll keep 'em in' -
Our LAW abiding citizens do think it meet and right
That curfew bell should still ring out at eight o'clock at night,
Perchance this ancient custom may bring good words to mind -
MAKE - PEACE before the sun goes down, to other's faults be
blind.
And so I'll end these little tales of good old Brackley folk
Hoping that those I've mentioned will appreciate a joke.

G.C.
May 1937.

57